My Loved One
Is Dying

My Loved One
Is Dying

John E. Biegert

The Pilgrim Press
Cleveland

lookingUp
Revised

The Pilgrim Press, 700 Prospect Avenue East
Cleveland, Ohio 44115-1100
thepilgrimpress.com

© 1990, 2004 by The Pilgrim Press

Interior design by Carrie Ann Ritchie.

Printed in the United States of America

15 14 13 12   5 4 3

ISBN 0-8298-1646-1

PREFACE

This booklet is written especially for you who are in the process of accepting or who have accepted the reality that a person who is dear to you is dying. Your loved one may be hospitalized at this time or is being cared for at home. Perhaps you are involved in a home hospice program or a hospice program provided by a hospital or convalescent home. Whatever the case, you know that your spouse, your parent, your daughter or son, or another person who is a meaningful part of your life will not be physically present after a few more weeks or months have passed.

I write from a perspective gained from more than four decades of pastoral ministry and several years of involvement as the clergy member of three interdisciplinary hospice teams, two which provide home hospice care, the other which offers hospice care in a convalescent home setting. It is my hope and prayer that the scriptural passages, thoughts, and prayers that follow will inform, strengthen, and comfort you as you walk with your loved one through the valley of the shadow of death.

> For everything there is a season, and a time for every matter under heaven:
> a time to be born, and a time to die; a time to plant, and a time to pluck
> up what is planted; . . . a time to weep, and a time to laugh; a time to
> mourn, and a time to dance.
>
> —ECCLESIASTES 3:1–2, 4

I do not believe, as did the Old Testament author of the above
words, that our lives are planned or mapped out in advance by God.
I do not believe that our Creator has selected a particular time when
your loved one will die. These verses from Ecclesiastes are important
to me, nonetheless, because they remind me of the realities that are
a part of life. To live is to experience good times and bad, times of
joy and times of sorrow. There are occasions that make us laugh, but
there are also occasions that make us cry. One of life's realities that
brings us sorrow and tears is the reality of death. None of us will
live forever. Death comes too soon to some, and not soon enough to
others. But death eventually comes. You have accepted the fact or are
in the process of coming to grips with the reality that your loved one
is dying. Know that God somehow will fill you with strength needed
for the days that lie ahead.

Loving God, I know that _____ is dying. Even though I know
that death comes to us all, I need your presence and help as I go
through this experience. Thank you for your promises that you
never will forsake me and that your strength will be sufficient for
today and for all of my tomorrows.

AMEN.

And you will know the truth, and the truth will make you free.

—John 8:32

All too often, when a loved one is dying, family members and friends fall into the trap of game playing with the dying person. Perhaps you believe that it will be easier for everyone if death is not talked about in the presence of your loved one who is dying. If so, the reality that is on everyone's mind is swept under the rug.

This avoidance or denial makes meaningful and honest communication virtually impossible between you and your dying loved one. You think that you will upset _____ if you talk about death, and _____ thinks that you will be upset if [she/he] talks about death. It has been my experience that nearly every terminally ill person knows that death is imminent. To try to hide this fact when in the presence of a dying person might only make [her/him] feel worse because [she/he] feels that you do not care enough to talk about what will, at times, be paramount in [her/his] mind—the fact that [she/he] is dying. Being truthful about the reality confronting you and your loved one will free both of you to share your deepest feelings of both love and sorrow with one another.

Help me, O God, to know that it is all right to talk to _____ about death. Then I can tell _____ how much [she/he] is loved, we can recall our happy times together, and we can cry together because we eventually will be separated from one another.

Amen.

Your Loved One Will Be with God

We do not live to ourselves, and we do not die to ourselves. If we live, we live to the LORD, and if we die, we die to the LORD; so then, whether we live or whether we die, we are the LORD's.

—ROMANS 14:7–8

The Christian faith affirms that death does not have the final word in life. You, therefore, can take comfort from the fact that your loved one, even after death, will continue to live with God and within you. What life after death will be like, none of us knows. However, we can affirm the words of John Greenleaf Whittier:

"Within the Maddening Maze of Things"

Within the maddening maze of things,
When tossed by storm and flood,
To one fixed trust my spirit clings;
I know that God is good!

I know not where his islands lift
Their fronded palms in air;
I only know I cannot drift
Beyond his love and care.

I know not what the future hath
Of marvel or surprise,
Assured alone that life and death
His mercy underlies.

Loving God, I don't know how it happens or what it will be like, but thank you for the fact that _____ will continue to live with you after [she/he] dies. Just as [she/he] will live with you, I know that _____ will continue to live on in me as I keep my memories green.

AMEN.

FINAL ARRANGEMENTS

When it was evening, there came a rich man from Arimathea, named Joseph, who was also a disciple of Jesus. He went to Pilate and asked for the body of Jesus; then Pilate ordered it to be given to him. So Joseph took the body and wrapped it in a clean linen cloth and laid it in his own new tomb, which he had hewn in the rock. He then rolled a great stone to the door of the tomb and went away.

—MATTHEW 27:57–60

When your loved one dies, some final tasks will await you. In all likelihood you will want a service held to honor _____ 's life, and you will need to determine the disposition of _____ 's body. Remember that there is nothing unloving, irreverent, or callous about discussing and planning these arrangements before your loved one's death. In fact, [she/he] might wish to have input concerning these matters.

It will be easier for you in the long run if you (and others in your family, if you so desire) visit with your clergyperson and a funeral

10

director before death occurs to make initial preparations for a memorial service or funeral as well as decisions pertaining to burial or cremation. Even though you know that death is forthcoming, when _____ dies you will find yourself in a state of shock, and your grief will affect your decision-making abilities. So, for your own sake and the sake of others, deal with the arrangements that will need to be made before your loved one dies.

In addition to contacting your clergyperson and funeral director, you should retain an attorney for advice concerning the legal ramifications of your loved one's pending death. If no Last Will and Testament, Living Will, or Power of Attorney has been executed, seek a legal opinion concerning any or all of them.

O God, I have been taught to love you with my mind as well as my heart. I know that planning for what will occur when _____ dies never will be easy but that it will be even more difficult when that moment actually comes. While I am thinking more clearly, grant me the strength I need to deal with these matters now.

AMEN.

ANTICIPATORY GRIEF

How long, O LORD? Will you forget me forever? How long will you hide your face from me? How long must I bear pain in my soul, and have sorrow in my heart all day long?

—PSALM 13:1–2A

> Blessed are those who mourn, for they will be comforted.
>
> —MATTHEW 5:4

We know that death brings sorrow and grief. For years, psychologists and other students of human nature have told us that grief work is necessary and that a grieving person can expect to have feelings such as numbness, loneliness, anxiety, emptiness, guilt, anger, self-pity, depression, helplessness, and hopelessness. Grief can cause physical illness and can make us feel that we are losing our mind.

Often, a person who knows that a loved one is dying experiences anticipatory grief, beginning the grief process while the loved one is still alive. With death, there sometimes comes a sense of relief because you know that the long process of dying is over for your loved one—and for you. You might then experience guilt for feeling this relief, but this is normal and can be expected.

Even if you experience anticipatory grief, your grieving process will not end overnight or even within a few weeks or months. Grief work can take as long as two years. (An additional resource to help you work through your grief is a companion booklet that I have written in the Looking Up series, *When Death Has Touched Your Life.*)

Comforting and caring God, who hears me when I cry to you, you know how much I hurt and how sad I am that _____ is dying. Yet, I know that my grieving is good, for it releases the feelings that are within me and it also says that I love _____ and that [she/he] loves me.

 AMEN.

12

The Stages of Dying

Even though I walk through the darkest valley, I fear no evil; for you are with me; your rod and your staff—they comfort me.

—Psalm 23:4

Dr. Elisabeth Kübler-Ross, medical doctor, psychiatrist, and world-renowned thanatologist, has authored numerous books on understanding death and dying. In her classic book, *On Death and Dying,* she identifies five successive stages that many who are dying go through. She developed these stages after talking to hundreds of terminally ill people. Dr. Kübler-Ross observed that these stages occur in the following order: denial, anger, bargaining, depression, and acceptance.

Your loved one might experience some or all of these stages in the order they appear above or in a different progression. In fact, your loved one might move back and forth between stages, denying [her/his] death one day and accepting it the next. Do not be surprised if your loved one expresses any of the following sentiments, commonly felt in the various stages:

Denial: *No, not me!*

It can't be!

The doctor must be wrong!

Anger: *Why me?*

I'm too young to die!

Why am I being punished?

What did I do to deserve this?

Bargaining: *God, I promise to be a better person if I can just live.*

Doctor, I'm sure that if you can give me something to make food taste better, I'll get well.

Depression: *I just don't care anymore.*

I don't want any company today. I'd rather just be left alone.

Acceptance: *I'm ready for death.*

I'm not afraid to die.

I'm glad that I have been able to put all of my affairs in order.

Respect the feelings of your loved one, whatever they may be. [She/He] will not benefit by your refusal to accept how [she/he] feels at a given moment. Being a good listener and letting [her/him] share what [she/he] feels at the moment are two of the greatest gifts you can give.

O God, my refuge and my strength, sustain _____ and me as together we walk through the valley of the shadow of death. Help me understand that the path might not be straight and that it might contain many stumbling blocks. Undergird me when I falter. Pick me up when I fall. And somehow assure _____ and me that you are with us each step of the way.

AMEN.

— What Shall I Tell My Children or Grandchildren? —

> When I was a child, I spoke like a child, I thought like a child, I reasoned like a child.
>
> —1 Corinthians 13:11a

Perhaps you are a parent with a small child or children. Perhaps you have grandchildren, nieces, nephews, or neighborhood children whose lives are being affected by the fact that your loved one is dying. How can you best relate to them? What can you tell them that will be of the most help to them, both now and later? My thinking and feelings in this area have been influenced to a great degree by Edgar N. Jackson's excellent book *Telling a Child about Death*. This book is no longer in print, however, I am indebted to Dr. Jackson for many of the insights that follow.

There is no easy or foolproof formula to follow when it comes to talking with a child or answering a child's questions about death. Quite likely, even if you fail to say the "correct" words or give the "correct" answers, you still will be able to help a child work through his or her feeling in this area. However, if you keep in mind the following guidelines, you may feel more at ease and more secure about the issue.

You probably wonder, "When is the best time to talk about death with a child?" The answer is, when the child wants to talk about it. Sometimes adults try to answer questions that have not been asked and ignore questions when they actually are raised.

Even before this point in your life, the child you care about has undoubtedly had some contact with death. For example, perhaps a teacher's parent died. Or a television cartoon the child was watching may have been interrupted with a news bulletin about an airplane crash in which people were killed. A dead bird might have been found in the yard. A pet might have died. A car ride might have taken the child past a cemetery. Perhaps a close friend was killed in a car accident. The fact that your loved one is dying probably is not the child's first contact with death.

You must deal with questions about death when they arise. If children do not find an explanation that satisfies them, their imaginations may run wild. Even though a child in your home might not actually ask questions about death at this time, his or her questions likely are just beneath the surface. Family life is built around emotional experiences, and when anticipated death brings on feelings of grief within you, children are quick to sense this change in your emotions. To try to conceal these feelings is unwise, for children easily see through adult falseness. To deny children a reasonable interpretation of the events they sense, see, or hear about is to deprive them of insight and reassurance when it is most needed.

When you wonder what, specifically, you should tell a child about death, remember that there are no universal or pat answers. Each person is unique and has unique and personal feelings about death. It, therefore, will be necessary for you to answer questions or speak about death from your own experience or in the context from which the questions arise. You can, however, be aware of the level of interest in death and the various ways of responding to death that are most characteristic of children in different age groups, and what follows may help you deal with the matter.

Children around the ages of two or three have little comprehension of the meaning of death, and are unlikely to ask questions about it. They live in the present and have little understanding of time. But they are aware of emotional changes and thus should not be overlooked or ignored. While a rational or detailed explanation of death is uncalled for, these children will be helped by large doses of love and interest in them and the world as they know it. You can provide the warmth and reassurance that a child needs by holding him or her in your arms and talking calmly about the things she or he knows.

From three to five years of age, most children cannot realize that death is natural and final. To them, death is like sleep: you are dead; then you are alive again. Or death is like a trip: you are gone, and then you come back. Consequently, children of this age may seem to be rather callous about death, even the death of a member of their own family. They express immediate sorrow but soon seem to forget all about the death. Guard against making the child feel guilty for not grieving and for taking death so lightly. Do not reinforce their ideas that death is like sleep or a trip. Do not try to argue them out of their belief, but, should they ask, tell them that their loved one is dead—not sleeping or away.

The world of children has expanded when they reach the age of six or seven and are in school. They know more people, and they have a new feeling for time and distance. Yesterday and tomorrow have more meaning. However, the meaning of death is still too large an idea for them to grasp easily. They may be able to understand that they no longer will be seeing a loved one, but the finality of death may be out of their reach. They can, though, understand something of the nature of death by a simple analogy. For example, a child of this age can be told, "Grandpa is becoming old and his body is wearing out. He will still exist, but won't live in his body anymore." You also might assure the child that this does not mean that your loved one will be like a ghost who comes back to visit or haunt. These explanations leave the door open for growth in the child's thinking about death, do not deny the reality of death, and respect the child's ability to adjust to the physical absence of someone who has been a familiar part of his or her world.

By the time children are eight or nine years old, their capacity for grasping concepts has developed. At this age, they appear to be able to accept the idea that a particular person is dying, but most likely they will not accept death as something that eventually happens to everyone, especially not to themselves. Eight or nine-year-olds who have had religious training will have some idea of a soul. And although they may be unable to explain its meaning, they are increasingly aware that life has mysteries. So the mystery of death can be added to the other mysteries of life, and the child will understand that not all questions about death can be definitely answered. At this age, the relation of personality to the body has meaning, and the separation of body and spirit can be understood in functional terms. The analogy Jackson uses to explain what happens at death is that if a pianist leaves the piano, the music no longer will be heard as the two must go together.

Finally, when children reach the age of ten, eleven, or twelve, they recognize that death is inevitable for all persons, including themselves. They are now old enough for their minds to begin furnishing abstractions with meanings that have significance for them. Additionally, they can understand what the loss incurred by death will mean to others and what it will mean to them. At this age, children arrive at a rather mature idea of what death means physically and emotionally. They do not want it to occur, but they know that death and sorrow will come to everyone.

Consider two concluding issues with these age distinctions in mind. First, when you are asked to explain why or how death occurs, you will usually deal with the issues of accident, illness, or old age. In each instance, it is better to deal with the immediate causes rather than to attempt to give a philosophical or religious interpretation. Rarely can the latter be understood by or be helpful to a child, and it can have negative ramifications if she or he is told that an accidental or untimely death is God's will or a part of God's plan.

Thus, in talking about an accidental death, you can emphasize the need for good judgment, care, and protecting oneself against other people's mistakes. In discussing sickness as the cause of death, you can emphasize the limitations of scientific knowledge and medical treatment as well as the need for better preventive measures. And in talking about old age as the contributing factor to death, you can explain that the body eventually grows so old and worn out that it no longer can do its work.

In such cases, it is important to make certain that the child understands that someone who is dying of an illness or who was killed in an accident, does not mean that they, too, may soon die of that illness or be stricken by the same kind of fatal accident. Such reassurance will do much to lessen any anxiety the child might feel.

The second issue concerns the extent to which a child should participate in the last rites for a member of the family. This is a debatable topic and there are often differences of opinion, even in the same family. Certainly a child should not be *forced* to participate in the rites marking the end of life. And a child who does not seem old enough to comprehend what is transpiring should not be subjected to the ritual. On the other hand, a child who is mature enough to have strong feelings about wanting to attend should be allowed to do so. Prohibiting a child from attending would give the child the feeling of being shut out of something that had great meaning. This might be far more disturbing than the experience of sharing the loss and being a part of the family circle at such a trying and traumatic time.

"What should I tell a child about death?" It depends upon the child's age and the circumstances. If you are reluctant to look at death realistically or if you are anxious to spare a child the necessity of facing death realistically, you are likely to fall into the trap of confusing and disturbing a child even further by attempting to soften the blow or evade the issue. It is much better for you to deal with questions and give truthful answers with love and reassurance.

Gracious and loving God, _____'s death is difficult for me to face. And I know that it is not easy for _____ as well. Enable me to be as helpful as possible to _____ during these days. Grant me, I pray, the ability to listen carefully and to speak with insight as I deal with _____'s questions and feelings.

AMEN.

TAKE CARE OF YOURSELF

Teacher, which commandment in the law is greatest? He [Jesus] said to him, 'You shall love the LORD your God with all your heart, and with all your soul, and with all your mind. This is the greatest and first commandment. And a second is like it: You shall love your neighbor as yourself. On these two commandments hang all the law and the prophets.'

—MATTHEW 22:36–40

A basic Christian teaching is that we are to love God and that we do so when we love others. In both the Old and New Testaments, we are commanded to love our neighbor as ourselves. Unfortunately, people too often overlook the final phrase, "as yourself." Ours is a faith that teaches that each human being is unique and of value, and that includes you. This sometimes is difficult to remember, especially when you are caring for your loved one who is dying.

It is natural that during this final stage in _____'s life you want to spend as much time with and do as many things for [her/him] as possible. Because you love _____ more than anyone else, no one can give more tender and loving care than you. You must be realistic enough to recognize, however, that during these days you also must take care of yourself. You cannot be the sole caregiver twenty-four hours a day, seven days a week. You need the help of others—family, friends, nursing personnel, volunteers.

You should recognize that you cannot do everything yourself. Your willingness to call on others is a sign of strength, not a confession of weakness. It indicates that you realize that you are not a superhuman being. Furthermore, it reveals that you are astute enough to be aware that if you become ill as a result of exhaustion and/or your resistance is low, you will be unable to be of any help to _____. Remember, even professional health care personnel work only eight to ten-hour shifts in order to insure their physical and emotional well-being.

A nearly universal concern shared by people who are dying is what the dying process is doing to the primary caregiver—in other words, to you! Your loved one will be less anxious and more assured if [she/he] knows that you accept your limitations and are willing to accept the physical and emotional support that is available from others.

Caring and loving God, help me to be aware that you care about me as much as you care about my loved one who is dying. Give me the wisdom to know that I cannot do everything for _____

_____, nor can I be with [her/him] all of the time. Thank you for others who are ready and willing to relieve and help. Grant me the grace and strength to ask!

AMEN.

WHAT WILL DEATH BE LIKE?

LORD, you have been our dwelling place in all generations. Before the mountains were brought forth, or ever you had formed the earth and the world, from everlasting to everlasting you are God . . . For a thousand years in your sight are like yesterday when it is past, or like a watch in the night . . . Our years come to an end like a sigh. The days of our life are seventy years, or perhaps eighty, if we are strong; even then their span is only toil and trouble; they are soon gone, and we fly away.

—PSALM 90:1–2, 4, 9B–10

"What can I expect to happen when my loved one actually dies?" is a question asked by many. "Will he experience a lot of pain?" "Will there be a great deal of trauma?" Although no definite answer can be given to these questions, you might find reassurance that most deaths are relatively peaceful and calm. Usually it will seem as though your loved one has just fallen asleep. Breathing will slow down, respiration will become shallower, and eventually the heart will stop.

Remember that when a person is dying, hearing is the last sense to fail. Thus, even though your loved one may be unresponsive and seem to be asleep or comatose, [she/he] may well be able to hear and understand what you are saying. Do not hesitate, therefore, to share words of love and gratitude with your loved one when death seems near.

O God, who will care for my loved one in death as you have in life and with whom will _____ be when death finally comes? I commend _____ to you and thank you that [she/he] will continue to live with you and in me forevermore. Comfort and sustain me as I see _____'s life slowly ebb.

Amen.

Dealing with Family Difference

Do not think that I have come to bring peace to the earth; I have not come to bring peace, but a sword. For I have come to set a man against his father, and a daughter against her mother, and a daughter-in-law against her mother-in-law; and one's foes will be members of one's own household.

—Matthew 10:34–36

Jesus, to whom the preceding words are attributed, often taught by hyperbole (exaggeration to make a point). In this teaching, he asked that his followers' primary allegiance be to him. However, these words seem literally to describe what happens in some families when a loved one is dying.

Differences of opinion and friction among family members sometimes occur when they are confronted by a terminal illness. Some may argue for a more aggressive course of treatment; others may want only palliative care provided. Some may not feel that adequate care is being given; while others may feel that the best possible care is being given under the circumstances.

Finally, some decisions concerning the care of your loved one will have to be made by you, the principal caregiver. Should your decisions incur the disfavor of others, try not to take it personally. Instead, recognize that honest differences of opinion often exist and that total agreement in all areas sometimes cannot be achieved. In such cases, listen to and respect what others are saying or suggesting. As lovingly as possible, inform them that your best judgment must prevail and ask them, if possible, to understand your point of view and accept your decision. Remind them, too, that this is a time when each of you needs the love and support of one another and ask them to please not let your differences of opinion drive a wedge between any of you.

O God, give me the strength to differ from others and to stand up for what I believe is best for _____ when others seem to disagree with my decisions. I know that _____'s illness is putting a great strain on all of us, but I pray that it will not impair our love and support for one another.

AMEN.

Giving Your Loved One Permission to Die

For to me, living is Christ and dying is gain. If I am to live in the flesh, that means fruitful labor for me; and I do not know which I prefer. I am hard pressed between the two: my desire is to depart and be with Christ, for that is far better; but to remain in the flesh is more necessary for you.

—Philippians 1:21–24

The dying process for some people takes longer than necessary because they subconsciously struggle to hold on to life for the sake of another person. Often that other person is a spouse, child, parent, or similarly close family member. The dying person has the feeling that [her/his] loved ones are not ready for [her/him] to die—that they are not willing to let go.

There may come a time in your loved one's dying when the most loving and beneficial act on your part will be to say, "It's all right for you to die. You have my permission. I will miss you; I never will forget you, but I will be okay." These might be the words that your loved one has been waiting to hear.

O God, I don't want _____ to hold on to life just on my account. I will not be any more ready for [her/his] death in a few hours or days than I am now. Give me the strength, therefore, to tell _____ that [she/he] has my permission to die.

Amen.

CONCLUDING THOUGHTS

When we honestly ask ourselves which person in our lives means the most to us, we often find that it is those who, instead of giving much advice, solutions, or cures, have chosen rather to share our pain and touch our wounds with a gentle and tender hand. The friend who can be silent with us in a moment of despair or confusion, who can stay with us in an hour of grief and bereavement, who can tolerate not knowing, not curing, not healing and face with us the reality of our powerlessness, that is a friend who cares.

—HENRI NOUWEN

And life is eternal
And love is immortal
And death is only a horizon.
And a horizon is nothing but
The limit of one's sight.
Death is not extinguishing the light.
It is putting out the lamp
Because the dawn has come.

—ANONYMOUS

Let children walk with Nature, let them see the beautiful blendings and communions of death and life, their joyous inseparable unity, as taught in woods and meadows, plains and mountains and streams of our blessed star, and they will learn that death is stingless indeed, and as beautiful as life.

—JOHN MUIR